Cigarette Cal
Nottingham⌣.…⌣

Brian Lund

1. John Player & Sons' offices and factory on Radford Boulevard, pictured on a postcard published by C. & A.G. Lewis in the mid-1920's. This is the only postcard in the book!

2. The badge of the Sherwood Foresters. No. 28 in Gallaher's *Army Badges* series, issued in 1939. The stag in the centre of the badge was said to symbolise the area where Robin Hood *"carried on his good work."*

Designed and published by Reflections of a Bygone Age, Keyworth, Nottingham 1997

Printed by Adlard Print and Typesetting Services, Ruddington, Nottingham

ISBN 0 946245 69 X

A trio of Nottinghamshire players from the excellent Wills set of *Cricketers* from 1908.

JOHN GUNN (NOTTS.).

ALBERT W. HALLAM (NOTTS.).

T. WASS (NOTTINGHAMSHIRE).

3. John Gunn, card no. 13 in this excellent set, played for the county from 1896 to 1925 and was selected for six tests for England. For Nottinghamshire, he scored over 24,000 runs and took 1,242 wickets.

4. Albert W. Hallam played for Leicestershire and Lancashire before returning to play for his native county. The text on the reverse of card no. 36 praised him as *"undoubtedly the best medium-paced bowler in England in 1907."*

5. 'Topsy' Wass was a fast bowler, who, along with Hallam, helped secure the county championship for Notts in 1907. No. 18 in this Wills series.

INTRODUCTION

During some four decades, from the start of the twentieth century to the outbreak of World War Two, cigarette cards occupied a position of some importance and influence in Britain. Given away with (virtually) every packet of cigarettes was a coloured (or, occasionally, monochrome) piece of cardboard, usually measuring 68 x 36mm, which provided a picture and some informative text. The recipient of the gift could learn about football and cricket stars, recognise politicians and military heroes, or navigate his way from one end of the country to the other. Sport, the theatre, history, geography, cinema, architecture, wildlife: the catalogue of subjects chosen by the tobacco companies was almost limitless. Billed as educational and entertaining, the real purpose of these items was to induce brand loyalty. Ironically, the biggest group of collectors of cigarette cards was that very age-group that wasn't actually supposed to be smoking - but no doubt children's persistent requests to parents and relatives, and even strangers - *"got any cigarette cards, mister?"* became a national catchphrase - persuaded adults to favour a particular brand of cigarettes. Albums were also made available by the issuing companies to encourage card retention.

The most influential companies in the card-issuing field in Britain were Ardath, Carreras, Churchman, Gallaher, Hill, Lambert & Butler, Ogdens, Godfrey Phillips, John Player, and Wills. One of the famous early names, Taddy, only produced cards from 1897-1915, but the rarity of their issues has made them extremely valuable today.

Not surprisingly, the cards in the cigarette packets became collectors' items. They were exchanged enthusiastically by schoolboys, used as both counters and currency in playground games of chance, and acquired some respectability when the Cartophilic Society was founded in 1933 to bring together adults interested in the collection and study of cigarette cards. The Society still thrives today, and in the meantime has published lots of reference books to help collectors.

Other businesses than tobacco companies began to realise the potential of giving away cards with their products; the items provided free in packets of tea, chewing gum, confectionery (most famously, the sweet cigarettes manufactured by firms such as Barratt from the 1930's onwards) and other products are normally referred to as 'trade' cards, but come under the same collecting umbrella.

Cigarette card production was halted in 1939 because of the need to save paper, and the genre went out of fashion in Britain's post-war austerity, though tobacco companies resumed the practice of card insertion with cigar products in the 1970's. Trade cards, though, are still being issued in a variety of shapes and sizes, and not always with products: some are merely offered for sale as an item in their own right, which brings into question their cartophilic status.

This book in the *'Yesterday's Nottinghamshire'* series provides a glimpse of some of the cards that have been issued in the twentieth century relating to the county. Sport, personalities, military subjects, animals, places, and - of course - the Robin Hood legend - all find a place.

One of Nottingham's most famous names, John Player, bought William Wright's tobacco factory in 1877 and immediately registered the Nottingham Castle trademark that was to become so familiar. As the business grew, he planned a large factory in Radford, incorporating offices, production plants and warehousing, and employing over 1,000 people by 1898. Separate sports and social facilities were established on the road out to Aspley. John Player's sons John D. and William G. continued the family runing of the business. J.D. Player went to Nottingham High School and later became a benefactor of the school and various local charities.

Player's factory employed 4,500 workers by the time Imperial Tobacco Co. bought the name. Now the firm, still a major name in the tobacco industry, has a modern factory on the Lenton Industrial Estate.

Brian Lund
June 1997

G. WOLFE.

NOTTS FOREST.

T. MARRISON,

NOTTS FOREST.

S. HARDY
NOTTS FOREST

6. Taddy & Co. were one of the most famous early manufacturers of cigarette cards, and all their sets are highly-prized. In 1907, they issued a huge set of 595 *Prominent Footballers*, of which George Wolfe was one. He played for Forest from 1905-11 after coming from Swindon Town.

7. Thomas Marrison, born in Sheffield in 1881, played for Notts Forest from 1906-11 before going on to Oldham. Another in the same long series.

8. Samuel Hardy, from Gallaher's *Famous Footballers*, issued in 1926. The reverse of this card is also illustrated.

FRANCIS G. MORGAN
NOTTS FOREST

9. Francis Morgan, centre-half and Nottingham Forest captain, was featured as no. 20 in another Gallaher *Famous Footballers* series, this time of 100 cards, issued in 1925. Forest had been relegated from Division One the previous season.

FAMOUS
FOOTBALLERS
SERIES OF 50

No. 26
SAMUEL HARDY.

England's goal-keeper in eighteen International games, was born at Newbould, near Chesterfield, and began his football career as a centre-forward. Has been playing football for a quarter of a century, having been associated with Chesterfield, Liverpool, Aston Villa, and now Notts Forest. Gifted with all the attributes of a class goal-keeper, Hardy has always been especially good in the art of tuition, and though over 40 years of age is still guarding the breach in remarkably clever fashion.

N. BURTON

NOTTS FOREST

10. In 1923, Godfrey Phillips Ltd published almost 2,500 photographic cards of footballers. Forest's Noah Burton was featured as no. 24.

T. GRAHAM (NOTTINGHAM FOREST)

D. MARTIN (NOTTINGHAM FOREST)

W. P. THOMPSON
(NOTTINGHAM FOREST)

11. Wills's *Association Footballers* set of 50 came out in 1939, the second set of that title. Thomas Graham was no. 22 in the series. Born in Durham, he joined Nottingham Forest in 1928, and three years later played for England against France.

12. David Kirker 'Boy' Martin left Belfast Celtic for a huge fee to join Wolves before moving to Nottingham. He became an Irish international while still a teenager. Churchman's *Association Footballers* set of 50 was issued in 1939 as a follow-up to the first series of the previous year.

13. Schoolboy international William Potter Thompson played for Forest from 1922-36, and proved a superb right back for them. He is shown on no. 72 in John Player's *Footballers 1928-9* series, with the numbering system continued from a previous issue.

Gallaher's Cigarettes.

14. Gallaher's *Footballers in Action* set of 1927, with a cup-tie between Bolton and Notts Forest (2-2) at the City Ground featured as no. 40. The reverse is also shown here.

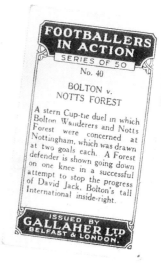

FOOTBALLERS IN ACTION

SERIES OF 50

No. 40

BOLTON v. NOTTS FOREST

A stern Cup-tie duel in which Bolton Wanderers and Notts Forest were concerned at Nottingham, which was drawn at two goals each. A Forest defender is shown going down on one knee in a successful attempt to stop the progress of David Jack, Bolton's tall International inside-right.

ISSUED BY
GALLAHER LTD
BELFAST & LONDON.

15. Notts County's Jack Cook played 117 games for the club between 1919 and 1923. No. 728 in the mammoth *Pinnace Footballers* series from Godfrey Phillips.

16. The following card in the series featured Frank Marriott, with the reverse also shown here.

WILLIAM ASHURST
NOTTS COUNTY

17. William Ashurst joined Notts County from Lincoln after spells at Leeds City and Durham. He was capped by England against Scotland in 1924-5 season. No. 82 in the Gallaher *Famous Footballers* series.

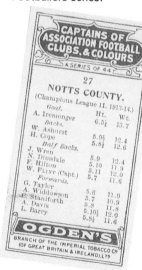

18. W. A. 'Billy' Flint appeared on Ogden's 1925 set of *Captains of Association Football Clubs & Colours.* Notts County's captain was no. 27 in the series; reverse also illustrated. From 1908-25, he played 416 games for Notts County, scoring 41 goals.

ALBERT IREMONGER
NOTTS COUNTY

19. Albert Iremonger was in the Notts County side of 1913-14 that was featured on the previous card. He was born at Wilford, made his debut for County in April 1904, and at 6′ 5″ was the tallest goalkeeper in the league at the time.

NOTTS COUNTY
TAKING THE FIELD F.B.40

20. Pattreioux of Manchester featured this photographic card (F.B. 40) as part of a *Footballers* set of 1928.

PLAYER'S CIGARETTES.

HARPER HENDRY
TOONE
BRAMLEY SHELTON
CALDERHEAD
WATSON DAFT
DONNELLY BRUCE
LOGAN

ASSOCIATION CUP WINNERS
NOTTS COUNTY. 1894.

21. Notts County won the F.A. Cup in 1894, beating Wanderers 4-1 at Everton. Their feat was commemorated in John Player's *Association Cup Winners* set of 50, issued in 1930.

J. RANKIN.

22. Scot J. Rankin joined Notts County in 1934, the year this set was issued, after spells with Dundee, Charlton Athletic and Chelsea. Ardath's *Famous Footballers* no. 10.

PLAYER'S
CIGARETTES

B. R. MILLS.
NOTTS COUNTY.

23. B.R. "Paddy" Mills came to Notts County from Hull City in 1926, and found a place in Player's *Footballers 1928* set of 50 cards.

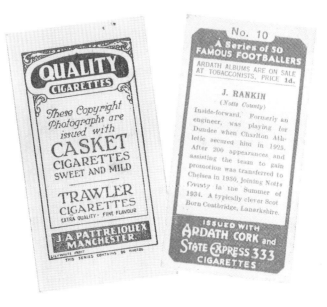

24. George Gunn, one of three county cricketers from the same family, appeared on a card in the Wills *Cricketers* 1928 set of 50. *"One of the most stylish batsmen in the country,"* enthused the caption, though George was by then in his 50th year. He toured Australia twice with the M.C.C.

25. This card of Ben Lilley comes from the same Wills series and features as card no. 29. Lilley was for many years understudy to the brilliant county wicket-keeper Thomas Oates.

26. Fred Barratt made his debut for Nottingham-shire in 1914, and combined aggressive fast bowling with big hitting. In 1927 he achieved the double (1,000 runs and 100 wickets), the first Notts player to claim the feat since John Gunn in 1906. Another card in the Wills 1928 *Cricketers* set.

28. Another Wills issue, this time with 'Vice Regal' pipe tobacco, appeared in 1911. Notts star Jimmy Iremonger featured as no. 59. Jimmy was an opening bat who played for the county between 1897 and 1914, and also played football for Nottingham Forest. He was the brother of Notts County footballer Albert *(see illus 19 and 46).*

27. Arthur Jones captained Notts in the Edwardian era, and scored 22,935 runs in a career spanning 22 years. He toured Australia in 1907-8.

J. HARDSTAFF (NOTTS.)

29. Joseph Hardstaff, no. 33 in Wills's *Cricketers* 1908 set of 50, issued just after a very successful tour to Australia. He played in 377 matches for Notts from 1902-6.

JOSEPH HARDSTAFF, JUN.

30. Joe Hardstaff jnr, a more complete player than his father, scored 83 centuries and over 31,000 runs for Notts between 1930 and 1955. Card no. 13 in Player's *Cricketers* 1938 set.

A. W. CARR.

31. Arthur Carr captained Notts and England, but had a controversial career, and was involved in the 'Bodyline' tour to Australia. Wills *Cricketers*, 2nd series of 50 (1929), card no. 9.

W. WHYSALL.

32. In the 1928 Wills *Cricketers* series, William Whysall is shown on card no. 48. He was a prominent member of the county side in the 1920's, opening the batting with George Gunn.

B. LILLEY. NOTTS.

33. John Player issued a set of *Caricatures by "Rip"* in 1926, and included wicket-keeper batsman Ben Lilley as card no. 24.

G. GUNN (NOTTINGHAMSHIRE).

34. George Gunn was already a well-established county and test player by the time Wills included him in their *Cricketers* series in 1908. The previous year he had headed the county averages.

35. Harold Larwood is possibly Nottingham-shire's best known crick-eter, partly because of the infamous 'Bodyline' tour to Australia in 1932-33. This Wills card, no. 28 in their 1928 *Cricketers* series, described him thus: *"below middle height and of medium physique, he takes a moderate run."*

36. Two years later, John Player were heralding him as *"England's best fast bowler"* on no. 30 in the *Cricketers* 1930 series. Larwood, born in 1904, had already had a decisive influence on an Ashes test and helped Notting-hamshire win the county championship in 1929.

37. By 1935, Larwood had shot to national fame outside cricket, and God-frey Phillips included him as no. 28 in their *In the Public Eye* set of cigarette cards. *"The world's fastest living bowler,"* the text eulogised, and emphasised his 33 wick-ets in the 1932-33 series.

38. Card no. 24 in Ardath's *Cricket, Tennis & Golf Celebrities,* issued in 1935.

39. British American Tobacco's 1926 photo-graphic issue of 25 *Eng-lish Cricketers* included Arthur W. Carr as no. 3. Carr had a 24-year career with Nottinghamshire until sacked in 1934.

40. Another card of Carr, one of Player's *Cricketers caricatures by "Rip"* from 1926. Carr was a forceful attacking batsman, and scored over 21,000 runs in his career.

42. Carreras issued a set of 50 *Famous Cricketers* in 1950 with their 'Turf' brand of cigarettes. No. 34 featured Reg Simpson, one of the county's most illustrious post-war players.

41. W.W. 'Dodger' Whysall played for Notts for 20 years from 1910, scoring over 21,000 runs and winning four test caps. This is no. 31 from a large series of 50 *Caricatures of Famous Cricketers* issued by R. & J. Hill with their 'Sunripe' cigarettes.

45. Wilfred Payton was a middle-order right hand bat who scored over 22,000 runs for Nottinghamshire between 1905 and 1931. This card is no. 63c in Godfrey Phillips' 'Pinnace' series of cricketers issued in 1924. There was a total of 198 cards in this series.

43. No. 15 in the same series was Walter Keeton. The cartoons were drawn by 'Dux' and a photograph of the player's head superimposed.

44. Bill Voce appeared on the same Ardath set as that shown in illus. 38. Voce took 1,558 wickets for the county from 1927-52 and was also at the centre of the 'Bodyline' controversy.

46. Player's *Footballers, Caricatures by "Rip".* Albert Iremonger was no. 16 in this 1926 set. The reverse text hailed him as *"the best goalkeeper who has never played for England."*

47. Robert Stewart Wallace featured as Nottingham Forest captain on no. 28 of Ogden's *Captains of Association Football Clubs & Colours*, published in 1926.

48. Notts County's centre-half of the early 1920's, Norman Dinsdale, featured as no. 11 of Player's *Football Caricatures by "Mac"* series of 1927.

49. Player's *Uniforms of the Territorial Army* was a set of 50 issued in 1939. Card no. 14 highlighted the Nottinghamshire Yeomanry, first raised in 1794.

50. No. 56 in Phillips' *Territorial Series* of 1908.

51. *Regimental Uniforms* was a series of 50 issued by Player in 1914. It shows a private of the 1st battalion of the Sherwood Foresters in 1748 uniform.

52. Godfrey Phillips issued a series of 126 G.P. Territorial Badges in 1913. The Sherwood Rangers featured as no. 3.

53. No. 121 in the same series.

PLAYER'S CIGARETTES.

Nottinghamshire Yeomanry. (Sherwood Rangers). (Hussars).

54. Player's *Drum Banners & Cap Badges* set of 50 appeared in 1924, with the Nottinghamshire Yeomanry (Sherwood Rangers, Hussars) as no. 26. The regiment was first raised in 1794, during the French Revolutionary War.

PLAYER'S CIGARETTES.

Nottinghamshire Yeomanry. (South Notts. Hussars). Now 107th (S, Notts. Hussars Yeomanry) Brigade, R.F.A. (2 Batts.).

55. The Nottinghamshire Yeomanry was officially formed in 1826 from a regiment of 'gentlemen and yeomanry' and became the South Notts Hussars in 1844. No. 35 in the same series.

56. The Robin Hood Rifle Volunteer Corps came into existence in 1859, with the first parade taking place at Nottingham Castle on May 30th that year. No. 11 in John Player's *Uniforms of the Territorial Army* shows an officer in front of the Exchange Building, and was issued in 1939.

57. Player's *Regimental Uniforms* no. 34, The Sherwood Foresters, shows a private in the 95th Derbyshire Regiment, which later became the 2nd Battalion Sherwood Foresters. In 1898, a black ram found at Kotah during the Indian Mutiny became the original regimental mascot, but drowned five years later in a well in Hyderabad.

58. This card is no. 35 in the *Regimental Colours & Cap Badges* set issued by John Player in 1910.

59. Another version of the same card from that series.

60. Gallaher's *Army Badges* series of 48 from 1939 included the Sherwood Foresters as card no. 28.

A selection of backs of military cards featured in the book

I should like to thank Tim and Shirley Ward of 'Put The Clock Back,' Paul Lynch of 'Kimberley Cards,' and Ted Wareham for the loan of cards, and the Imperial Tobacco Company for permission to reproduce material. Thanks, too, to Grenville Jennings for some of the sports detail.

Officer, 45th Foot.   1792

61. Player's *Regimental Uniforms* no. 32 (1912) showed an infantry officer of the 45th Foot, the Nottinghamshire Regiment, in 1792.

'THE DERBY RAM,'
REGIMENTAL PET OF THE SHERWOOD FORESTERS

62. Another of the long line of Derby rams, mascot of the Sherwood Foresters, on a Wills *Regimental Pets* set from 1911, given away with Scissors cigarettes.

Officer, 45th Foot. 1811.

63. Officer of the 45th Foot depicted at the time of the Peninsular Wars on card no. 33 of Player's *Regimental Uniforms.*

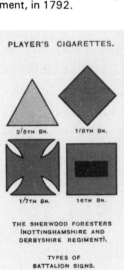

2/5TH BN.   1/6TH BN.

1/7TH BN.   16TH BN.

THE SHERWOOD FORESTERS
(NOTTINGHAMSHIRE AND
DERBYSHIRE REGIMENT).

TYPES OF
BATTALION SIGNS.

64. Player's *Army, Corps & Divisional Signs 1914-18* ran to two series totalling 150 cards issued in 1924-25. Thirty battalions of the Sherwood Foresters were involved in the First World War.

The late Pte. JACOB RIVERS, V.C.

65. Gallaher's *The Great War Victoria Cross Heroes* ran to eight sets of 25 cards, issued between 1915 and 1918. Jacob Rivers, of the 1st Battalion Sherwood Foresters, was honoured for exceptional bravery at Neuve Chapelle in March 1915, when he was killed protecting one of his battalion fronts.

Captain CHAS. G. VICKERS, V.C.

66. Charles Vickers, 7th Sherwood Foresters, won the V.C. at Hohenzollern in October 1915, when he was badly wounded defending a trench against heavy fire.

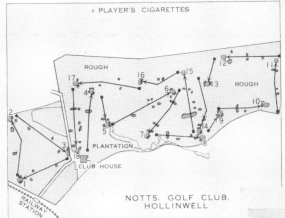

ROUGH

ROUGH

PLANTATION

CLUB HOUSE

NOTTS. GOLF CLUB, HOLLINWELL

RAILWAY STATION

67. Hollinwell Golf Club near Newstead Abbey was one of 25 courses featured on Player's *Championship Golf Courses* issued in 1936, when visitors could pop in for a round for five shillings.

68. Richard Parker Bonington (1801-28) is probably Arnold's most well-known figure: his name is remembered in the title of the town's theatre today. At the age of 15, he was already studying at the Louvre, and by the time of his early death, was recognised as one of the finest water-colour artists in England and France. His 'London Bridge' was no. 15 in Wills's *British School of Painting* series from 1927.

Wills's Cigarettes

"London Bridge."   R. P. Bonington.

69. One of several railway engines with names that have a Nottingham connection, 46251 City of Nottingham featured in the Player's Doncella cigars *Golden Age of Steam* set from 1976.

70. Robert H.T. Turner

71. Arthur O. Jones

72. Thomas W. Oates

Taddy & Co.'s cigarette cards are among the most sought-after of all by collectors, with many of the Taddy issues selling now for over £100 per card. In 1907, the company produced a set of 238 *County Cricketers*, five of which are featured here.

73. Wilfred Payton

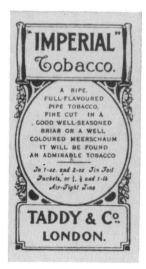

74. George T. Branston

GEORGE GREENWOOD

R. LYALL

75. George Greenwood rode for Nottingham's speedway team in 1933, 1936 and 1938, when he was captain. He appeared as no. 16 in Player's 1937 set of 50 *Speedway Riders*.

76. Nottingham Racecourse was the scene of jockey Robert Lyall's best achievement, when he rode three winners on the same afternoon at a 1930 meeting. Card no. 24 in Ogden's *Steeplechase Celebrities* from 1931.

77. Billiards and snooker champion Joe Davis was born in Whitwell in 1901 and became Britain's most famous performer on the tables. He was resident world snooker and billiards champion for much of the 1930's. R. & J. Hill's 1939 set *Celebrities of Sport* introduced Davis as card no. 25.

79. A. & B.C. chewing gum *All Sport* series of 1954 featured 120 stars, including Nottingham Panthers ice-hockey player Chick Zamick.

78. D.E. Woods, research worker in bio-chemistry at Nottingham University, won the King's Prize at Bisley in 1934. Gallaher's *Champions* series.

Presented by A. & B.C. CHEWING GUM LTD.

CHICK ZAMICK
Nottingham Panthers Ice Hockey Star

No. 35   "All Sport" Series

CYRIL STAPLETON
in
"The Melody Dances"

© TVP Ltd

80. Cyril Stapleton led one of the most popular dance bands of the 1950's. Born in Nottingham, he was a child prodigy on violin and played in Henry Hall's BBC orchestra while a teenager. No. 44 in A. & B.C. gum's *Who-z-at star* series, issued in 1958.

WILLS'S CIGARETTES

FOSTER RICHARDSON

WILLS'S CIGARETTES

BILLY MERRIN

81. Radio star Billy Merrin was born in Nottingham in 1900 and worked as a clerk in a local warehouse before music took over his life. In the 1930's he became a famous band-leader, making his first broadcast in 1932. This card featured in Wills's 2nd series of *Radio Celebrities* of 1934.

82. Nottingham-born Foster Richardson grew up on a farm, but his talent for singing got him a scholarship at the Royal Academy of Music. He sang bass in Sir Thomas Beecham's opera company and made his first radio appearance in 1927. No. 16 in the 2nd *Radio Celebrities* series from Wills.

83. Lord Byron is one of Nottinghamshire's most famous sons, celebrated for poetry and romance. His home was Newstead Abbey, though he did not actually live there for long. Typhoo Tea issued a set of 25 Houses of *Famous Men* in 1934, with Newstead as no. 3.

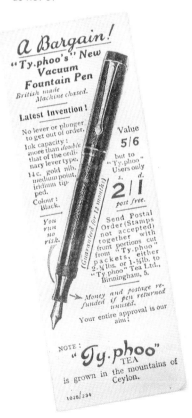

84. Maggie Eaton, born in Nottingham, was one of the glamorous performers at the Windmill Theatre in London in the 1930's. This card is one of a huge series of *Photocards* issued by Ardath from 1936-9.

Wills's Cigarettes

The Flying Horse, Nottingham

85. Wills's *Old Inns* included "The Flying Horse" at Nottingham as no. 10 in a 40-card series issued in 1936. The name of the inn came from the mythological Pegasus, and the building seen here dated from Elizabethan days. The facade remains, but the interior is no more, and a shopping arcade has replaced the stylish rooms of the inn.

86. A second series of *Old Inns* featured "Ye Olde Trip to Jerusalem" as card no. 40. One of the various establishments that claim to be the oldest inn in England, the "Trip" is one of Nottingham's top tourist attractions.

Wills's Cigarettes

Ye Olde Trip to Jerusalem, Nottingham

Wills's Cigarettes

Ye Olde Bell, Barnby Moor, Nottinghamshire

87. "Ye Olde Bell" on the Great North Road near Retford found greatest fame from its landlord from 1800-42: George Clark was a racehorse breeder with over 100 horses in his stables. The inn became a private residence for 60 years after the decline of coaching, but it re-opened in 1906. 1st series of *Old Inns*, no. 39.

88. Gallaher's *Interesting Views* no. 94 (of 100) showed Nottingham Castle. Issued in 1923, the black & white photographic cards are a departure from the cigarette card norm of coloured, artist-drawn examples.

89. Cope Bros. of Liverpool and Richard Lloyd of London jointly issued a 25-card set of *Castles* in 1939. The famous Newark structure where King John died and Charles I surrendered during the Civil War featured as no. 19.

90. Clumber's Italian Garden's were represented as card no. 9 on Wills's 1930 set *Beautiful Homes*. The house was built towards the end of the 18th century for the 2nd Duke of Newcastle.

91. No. 20 in the same series showed Newstead Abbey, originally founded as a priory in the 12th century. Sir John Byron acquired the abbey after the dissolution of the monasteries and adapted it as a residence.

WILL'S CIGARETTES

BOROUGH ARMS.
MANSFIELD.

92. Mansfield featured as no. 113 on Wills's 3rd series of *Borough Arms*. There were 200 of these cards in total in the four series. The reverse text highlighted the origin of the various emblems, including the oak tree representing Sherwood Forest.

WILL'S CIGARETTES

LAUDA FINEM.

SCHOOL ARMS.
NOTTINGHAM HIGH SCHOOL.

93. Wills issued a 50-card set of *School Arms* in 1906, with Nottingham High School, founded in 1513 by Dame Agnes Mellors, as no. 23.

BESTWOOD LODGE, NOTTS.

AUSPICIUM MELIORIS

Player's Cigarettes

94. *Country Seats and Arms* was issued in three series of 50 cards by John Player in 1909-10. Bestwood Lodge, now fire brigade headquarters and a hotel, was built as the seat of the Duke of St. Albans, son of Charles II.

THORESBY PARK, NOTTS.

Player's Cigarettes

95. Thoresby Park, no. 84 in the same series, was the seat of Earl Manvers. The first Earl was Charles Medows, three of whose ancestors had held the office of Knight Marshal of the King's Palace.

No 113 SECOND EDITION

WILL'S Cigarettes

MANSFIELD.
(Borough Arms.)

The Saxon cross commemorates the fact that Mansfield was a royal manor in the Confessor's time. The cotton banks are an allusion to the local industry of cotton-doubling, while the oak tree represents Sherwood Forest. All the other emblems are from the ... of families ... the town ... ...vendish ...osslets, ... Mans- ...stry ...

SECOND SERIES 84

EARL MANVERS.

The first Earl Manvers was Charles Medows, whose uncle, grandfather, and great grandfather each held the office of Knight Marshal of the King's Palace. He succeeded to the estates of another uncle, the second and last Duke of Kingston, and assumed the name and arms of Pierrepont. The mother of the present Earl was the daughter of the Duc de Coigny of France. His motto means, "Repose with quiet confidence."

ISSUED BY THE
JOHN PLAYER & SONS

BRANCH OF THE IMPERIAL TOBACCO CO.
OF GREAT BRITAIN & IRELAND, LTD.

NOTTINGHAM

96. *Country Seats and Arms* 2nd series: no. 63 Rufford Abbey, seat of Lord Savile.

Welbeck Abbey

Clumber

Chapel Bar, Nottingham

100. Southwell was founded as a bishopric in February 1884, and its arms featured as card no. 46 in *Arms of the Bishopric*, a set produced by Wills in 1907.

97. The Duke of Portland was rewarded with Welbeck Abbey by William of Orange when he became William III in 1688. The third duke assumed the name and arms of Cavendish, whose snake crest features on this card, no. 49 in the first *Country Seats and Arms* series.

98. The Duke of Newcastle traced his descent from the Clinton family, whose crest was a plume of feathers. The peacock represents the Pelham family name, which was assumed by the second duke. Card no. 37 in the 1st series.

99. Chapel Bar in Nottingham survived until 1743, the rooms beneath it housing a guardroom and chapel. Towards the end of its use, the buildings were used as a brewhouse and part of the roof was turned into a garden. Card no. 32 in John Player's *Celebrated Gateways*, a set of 50 issued in 1909.

101. John Player and Raleigh are two of the city's most famous business names, so it was appropriate that the tobacco firm should issue a *Cycling* set in 1939. This card gave details of Youth Hostel Association membership and accommodation for cyclists: *"members can stay for 1/- a night, cooking facilities being provided for those carrying their own food."* The picture shows Hartington Hall hostel in Dovedale.

102. Raleigh issued their own set of cards in 1957 as an advertising promotion. This is the Trent Sports for ladies.

THIS SURFACE IS ADHESIVE. ASK YOUR
TOBACCONIST FOR THE ATTRACTIVE
ALBUM (PRICE ONE PENNY) SPECIALLY
PREPARED TO HOLD THE COMPLETE SERIES

CYCLING

A SERIES OF 50
BY THE EDITOR OF "CYCLING"

41

CYCLISTS AND THE Y.H.A.

Cyclists and walkers of both sexes may join the Youth Hostels Association (England and Wales) for 2/6d. a year under the age of 25, or 5/- for those 25 and over. The same subscriptions apply to the Scottish Y.H.A., but the age limit for 2/6d. is 20. There are nearly 300 hostels in England and Wales and over 50 in Scotland where members can stay for 1/- a night, cooking facilities being provided for those carrying their own food. The war-iens of many hostels also supply cooked meals, average prices being 1/- per meal. We show Hartington Hall Hostel, Dovedale, in the Peak District.

JOHN PLAYER & SONS
BRANCH OF THE IMPERIAL TOBACCO CO.
(OF GREAT BRITAIN & IRELAND) LTD.

103. The Sports Tourist for ladies from the same set.

John Player detailed exactly how their cigarettes were produced on a 1926 set, From Plantation to Smoker, of 25 cards.

104. Card 14 - Unloading tobacco at an Imperial Tobacco Company factory. These plants examined the raw material , re-dried it, and packed it for export to Britain.

105. A handstemming room featured on card 17. Here the stem was removed from the leaf before re-drying.

106. A John Player factory on card 24. The text reverse is shown below.

107. The finished product appears on the final card in the set, which shows girls putting cigarettes into trays as they pour out of the machine. They were then packed into the familiar lifebuoy packet.

FROM PLANTATION TO SMOKER
A SERIES OF 25

25
A Cigarette Machine Room.
Here we see a room filled with cigarette machines. Each machine is run by a highly skilled operator, and a girl whose duty it is to put the cigarettes into trays as they pour out of the machine preparatory to the ...ing packed into the fan ...
packet: Ove...
employed in...
of Player's ...
and Cigar...

JOHN...
BRANCH
(OF G...

FROM PLANTATION TO SMOKER
A SERIES OF 25

24
A Cutting Room.
This illustration shows semi-manufactured cigarette tobacco in one of John Player & Sons' Factories. The leaf after being carefully blended is cut on a high speed machine capable of cutting many hundreds of pounds a day. After standing a few days to ensure the various grades blending together, the cut tobacco is sent in tin trolleys to the cigarette-making machines..

ISSUED BY
JOHN PLAYER & SONS
BRANCH OF THE IMPERIAL TOBACCO CO
(OF GREAT BRITAIN & IRELAND) LTD

MITCHELL'S CIGARETTES

ERROL FLYNN (FIRST NATIONAL)

WILLS'S CIGARETTES

CLUMBER SPANIEL

108. Errol Flynn in the 1937 film version of *The Adventures of Robin Hood*, no. 11 in the 25-card set from Stephen Mitchell & Son in 1939, *Stars of Screen & History*.

110. The 1937 Wills set of *Dogs* was based on paintings by Arthur Wardle. No. 32 was the Clumber Spaniel, with the characteristics of the breed on the reverse.

PLAYER'S CIGARETTES.

FARMER UNLOADING TOBACCO AT SALES WAREHOUSE.

111. Card no. 12 in the Player *From Plantation to Smoker* series.

ROBIN HOOD & HIS MERRY MEN. "Typhoo" CUT-OUT SERIES OF 30.

Nº 1 ROBIN HOOD.

109. The cards in Typhoo Tea's 1928 set of 30 *Robin Hood and His Merry Men* were intended to be cut out and used as free-standing models (the instructions were on the reverse). No. 1 showed the great man himself.

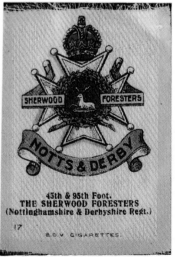

SHERWOOD FORESTERS

NOTTS & DERBY

45th & 95th Foot.
THE SHERWOOD FORESTERS
(Nottinghamshire & Derbyshire Regt.)

17

B.D.V. CIGARETTES.

112. Godfrey Phillips' silk issue of *Regimental Colours & Crests* in 1915, given away with B.D.V. cigarettes, included the Notts & Derby crest as no. 17.

113. King Charles I's raising of the royal standard at Nottingham in 1642 was rated worthy of inclusion in Typhoo's 1938 set *Interesting Events in British History.*

114. Lord Howard of Effingham, hero of the defeat of the Spanish Armada in 1588, was created Earl of Nottingham in 1597. Two years later, he became supreme commander of the English army and navy. No. 61 in the *Celebrities and their Autographs* set issued by Nicholas Sarony & Co. (Cigarette Card specialists) of New Bond Street, London in 1923.

115. Another card of the Earl in J. Wix & Son's *Builders of Empire* 50-card issue from 1937, given away with Kensitas (*"the mild cigarette - just what the doctor ordered"*). Reverse text notes the Earl as *"a man of courageous action and a dependable adviser .... a mainstay of England during the years when the foundations of the British Empire were laid."*

116. King John features large in Nottinghamshire legend through the Robin Hood connection, but more certain is the fact that he died at Newark Castle on 19th October 1216, in his 50th year. The coats of arms of John and his second wife Isabella of Angouleme are shown on card no. 7 in Lambert & Butler's *Arms of Kings & Queens of England* (1906).

117 - 119. Three cards from the Typhoo cut-out series (others appear in illus. 109 and 121).

If you are interested in collecting cigarette or trade cards, the following contacts may be useful:

* Cigarette card fairs, with some 15-25 national dealers attending, are held regularly at two local venues, Harvey Hadden Sports Centre and Silverdale Community Centre. Ring Mary Lund on 0115-937-4079 for details of the first venue; David Hunter on 0115-937-6985 about the latter venue.

* A magazine for card collectors, *Card Times*, is published monthly. Ring David Stuckey on 01695-423470 for subscription details.

* Sales of cigarette cards are held regularly in Nottingham by Trevor Vennett-Smith auctions. Details and dates from 0115-983-0541.

* The shop Collectors' World at 188 Wollaton Road, Nottingham, carries a range of collectable cards for sale.

* Albums for cigarette cards are available at Nottingham Stamp Centre, 3 Wollaton Street, Theatre Square, Nottingham.

* *Cigarette Card Values* is an annual catalogue listing all cards with current prices. Contact Martin Murray on 0181-202-5688. Murraycards is also a leading retailer of cigarette and trade cards.

If you have any other questions on the hobby, contact the publishers of this series of books at the address on the back cover.

120. Give-away cards with chewing gum were immensely popular in the 1950's. The Master Vending Co. Ltd offered a set of 25 in 1958 with the imaginative title *A Bombshell for the Sheriff*. The reverse featured a cartoon strip which was continuous through the series.

THE DEATH OF ROBIN HOOD

121. No. 10 in the Typhoo cut-out series shows the villain of the Robin Hood legend, the Sheriff of Nottingham. Reverse text goes so far as to identify him as either Ralph Murdach (sheriff in 1189) or William Brewerre (1194).

122. Robin Hood's adventures allegedly took him far beyond Sherwood Forest, and the location of his death is often quoted as being at Kirklees Priory in West Yorkshire. Churchman's *Legends of Britain* 1936 set illustrated on card no. 29 Robin's last request - *"bury me where the arrow falls."*

123. Ogden's *Sectional Cycling Map* series of 1910 split Nottinghamshire into two parts, with the northern half on card 18. The reverse text was the same on each card in the set.

124. No. 22 in that same Ogden's series, featuring South Nottinghamshire.

125. Lambert & Butler issued a *Find Your Way* set of 50 cards in 1932. Three different varieties were available, including a red overprint on the back (illustrated below). Six routes were involved, and collectors were invited to enter a simple competition, once they had amassed the whole set, to win a pocket road atlas.

FIND YOUR WAY!

SERIES OF 50   CARD No. 27

This Series of 50 covers 6 main routes in England and Wales, viz.:

ROUTE A, LONDON - EXETER   ROUTE D, BIRMINGHAM - BOURNEMOUTH
    „   B. LONDON - MANCHESTER   „   E. BRISTOL - LEEDS
    „   C. LONDON - SCARBOROUGH   „   F. CARDIFF - LIVERPOOL

We invite you to collect this Series and find the numbers of the cards that make up these 6 routes. Write them in correct order on Card No. 50 provided for this purpose, also your name and address IN BLOCK LETTERS, and send complete set of fifty, SECURELY PACKED to:

LAMBERT & BUTLER, Box No. 152, Drury Lane, London, W.C.2

In exchange you will receive, post free, a complete Pocket Road Atlas of England and Wales.

Ask your Tobacconist for Chart—it will interest and help you.

ISSUED BY THE IMPERIAL TOBACCO COMPANY OF GREAT BRITAIN AND IRELAND, LIMITED.

126. Photographic viewcards were not as common on cigarette cards as they were on picture postcards, but an exception was Gallaher's 1910 issue of *English and Scotch views.* This card of Nottingham Market Place, card no. 10 in the series, shows the covered market stalls.

127. Trent Bridge looking west - no. 39 in the same series.

128. Card no. 40: Nottingham Market Place, with Queen Victoria's statue, unveiled in 1905, prominent in the background.

129. The lake at the Arboretum on card no. 59.

SUSPENSION BRIDGE, NOTTINGHAM

130. R. & J. Hill issued five series of 48 *Views of Interest* in 1938-39, and included the Suspension Bridge over the River Trent, connecting Victoria Embankment with West Bridgford. It was built in 1906.

DUKERIES

131. Pattreioux's *Sights of Britain* (1st series, 1936) were given away with 'Senior Service' cigarettes. Card no. 41 was a photographic view of the famous 'Major Oak' in Sherwood Forest.

The cards in this book represent only a small selection of those available on Nottinghamshire themes and personalities. See information after caption 119 for advice on how to build up a collection.

SIGHTS OF BRITAIN

SERIES OF 48

No. 41

Dukeries

A lovely district in the north-west of Nottinghamshire forming part of Sherwood Forest, so named because of the large number of ducal seats found here, and rendered doubly fascinating by its historical associations. The finest of all the old forest trees is shown in this photograph, the "Major Oak," a splendid specimen of huge dimensions, the hollow of which will hold twenty persons. This part of the far-famed Sherwood Forest was the haunt of the far-famed Robin Hood and his merry men, whose "larder"—another great hollow oak—is still to be seen.

These interesting Photographs are issued with the following Cigarettes :-
SENIOR SERVICE....10 FOR 6ᵈ 20 FOR 1/-
JUNIOR MEMBER....25 FOR 1/-
ILLINGWORTH'S Nº 10...

NOTTINGHAM CASTLE

132. Card no. 83 in Hill's 2nd *Views of Interest* series - hand-coloured - was Nottingham Castle, restored after it was extensively burned by rioters in 1831.

NOTTINGHAM

133. An unusual view of the Market Square on card 19 of Pattreioux's *Britain from the air* series of 1939.

134. From the same manufacturer came a *Winter Scenes* series in 1937. One of the cards showed a spot near Southwell which was alleged to have been a source of inspiration to the poet Lord Byron.

BYRON'S POOL

137. Arthur Wardle paintings appeared on both postcards and cigarette cards. This was no. 11 of Player's 1933 *Dogs* series, one of several issuing this artist's work.

135. The Clumber Spaniel takes its name from Clumber Park, seat of the Duke of Newcastle. This trio featured on card no. 24 of Carreras' *Dogs & Friend* series of 50 photographic cards of 1936.

CLUMBER SPANIEL

138. Clumber Spaniels grew to 12-14 inches in height, with a weight of 55-75 pounds. Ogden's *Dogs* (1936) included the breed as no. 30 in their set.

Spaniel Clumber.

136. The firm of Moustafa Ltd was based in Piccadilly, and only ever issued five sets of cards, between 1923 and 1925. These Leo Chambers *Dogs Heads* appeared as a set of 40 - this was no. 35. The text recommended Spratt's dog food.